THE ROLLING ST

BEGGARS BANQUET

ALBUM NOTES

Release Date: November, 1968

Top Chart Position: No. 5, reached January 11, 1969

Standout Tracks: "Sympathy for the Devil," "Street Fighting Man," "No Expectations" and "Salt of the Earth"

Significance: Signified a return to the band's blues roots, forsaking psychedelic experimentation; included songs with social and political commentary that reflected the political turbulence of 1968; incorporated world music elements such as African rhythms in "Sympathy for the Devil."

Milestone: Considered among the greatest blues-based rock albums of all time.

Alfred Publishing Co., Inc.
16320 Roscoe Blvd., Suite 100
P.O. Box 10003
Van Nuys, CA 91410-0003
alfred.com

ISBN-10: 0-7390-4161-4
ISBN-13: 978-0-7390-4161-1

FOREWORD

At the time of its release at the end of 1968, *Beggars Banquet* was widely hailed as a return to form for the Rolling Stones. *Their Satanic Majesties Request*, released the previous year, was thought to be a noble, but not entirely successful, experiment. Leaving the ethereal and psychedelic behind, the band first entered London's Olympic Studios in March with American producer Jimmy Miller, who had previously worked with The Spencer Davis Group and Traffic. *Beggars Banquet* would be Brian Jones' last hurrah with the band prior to his departure and subsequent death. His role in the band had been diminishing, but he is heard playing slide guitar on "No Expectations," harmonica on "Dear Doctor" and "Prodigal Son," tamboura on "Street Fighting Man," and Mellotron on "Stray Cat Blues."

The album's undisputed and eternal touchstone is its first track, "Sympathy for the Devil." Together with track one ("Street Fighting Man") on the original vinyl album's second side, "Sympathy for the Devil" encapsulated the political and social turbulence that swept through Western Europe and Britain at the time. The African rhythms and overtly satanic lyric content of "Sympathy" were the perfect musical underbed for the era. "Street Fighting Man" became the battle cry of the student uprisings that swept the European continent, the United States and Mexico; the Stones had provided the soundtrack for a revolution, it seemed.

Acoustic blues resonate through the album with the poignant "No Expectations" and anthemic "Salt of the Earth." The only non-original on the album is "Prodigal Son"—a rootsy, honest reworking of Reverend Robert Wilkins' song that was first recorded in Memphis in 1929. It's an earthy delight that includes guitar work from Ry Cooder. "Stray Cat Blues," with its sleazy theme of underage cheap thrills, reinforces the band's bad boy image in a most shocking and, perhaps, tongue-in-cheek way.

From a visual perspective, the album has resonated through the decades. The sessions were documented by French new-wave director Jean Luc Godard in the film *One Plus One* that was retitled *Sympathy for the Devil* in recognition of the power of the song. The album cover became almost as big a cause célèbre as the provocative songs it was meant to package. The band's choice was a shot of a raunchy toilet stall festooned with graffiti (one note reads "BOB DYLAN'S DREAM," with an arrow pointing to the flush handle). Both the U.K. (Decca) and U.S. (London) labels rejected the art and a standoff ensued with the band that delayed the release. Ultimately, a simple mock invitation in a florid script was used but the rawness of the music powered through the sanitized cover art.

Beggars Banquet proved to be a career landmark for the Rolling Stones. The songs confirmed the Jagger/Richards team preeminence in the field of primal, blues-based rock that would stand for all time.

THE ROLLING STONES

BEGGARS BANQUET

CONTENTS

SYMPATHY FOR THE DEVIL

Words and Music by
MICK JAGGER and KEITH RICHARDS

Verse:

1. Please al-low me_ to in-tro-duce my-self,_ I'm a man of wealth and taste.

I've been a-round_ for a long,_ long year,_ stole man-y a man's_ soul_ and faith._

2. See additional lyrics

I was a-round when Je - sus Christ_ had his mo-ment of doubt and

pain. Made damn_ *Chorus:* that Pi - late washed his hands and sealed his

fate._

Pleased to meet_ you,_____ hope you guess_ my

6

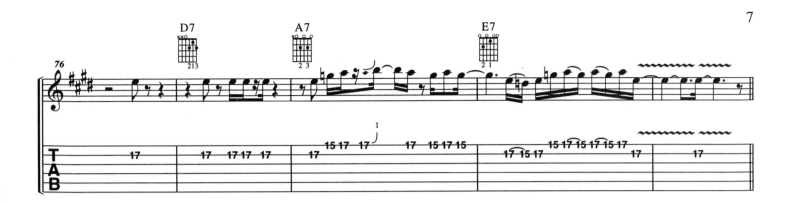

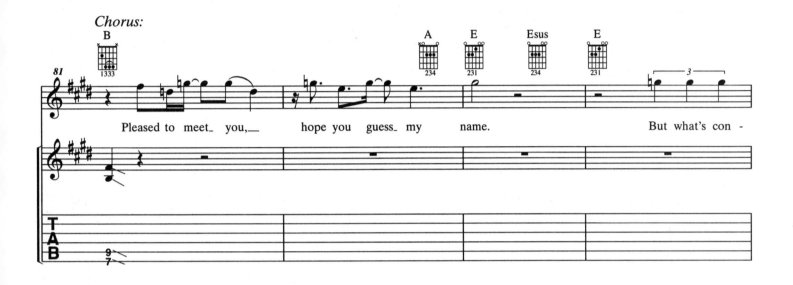

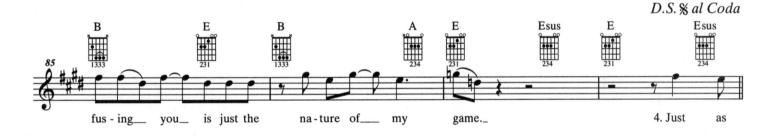

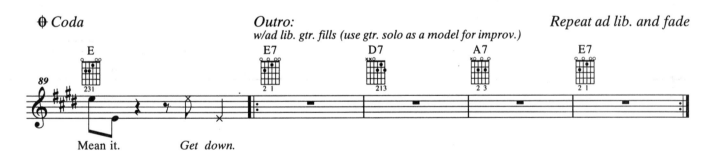

Verse 2:
Stuck around Saint Petersburg
When I saw it was a time for a change.
Killed the Tzar and his ministers;
Anastasia screamed in vain.
I rode a tank, held a general's rank
When the blitzkrieg raged and the bodies stank.
(To Chorus:)

Verse 4:
Just as every cop is a criminal
And all the sinners, saints.
As heads is tails, just call me Lucifer
'Cause I'm in need of some restraint.
So if you meet me, have some courtesy,
Have some sympathy and some taste.
Use all your well learned politesse
Or I'll lay your soul to waste.
(To Chorus:)

NO EXPECTATIONS

Words and Music by
MICK JAGGER and KEITH RICHARDS

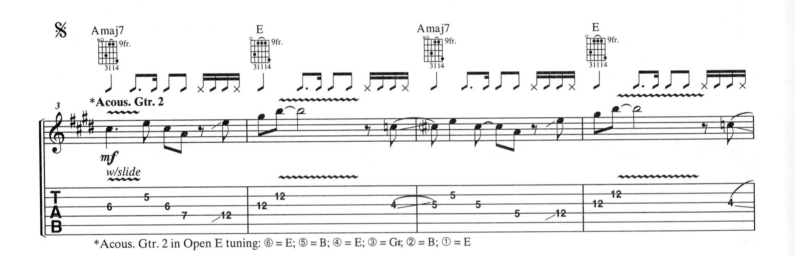

*Acous. Gtr. 2 in Open E tuning: ⑥ = E; ⑤ = B; ④ = E; ③ = G♯; ② = B; ① = E

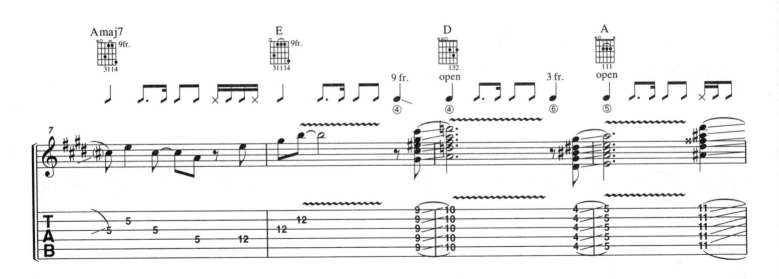

No Expectations - 3 - 1
25774

4. Our

Verse:

Acous. Gtr. 1 cont. simile

1. Take me to_____ the sta - tion and put me on_____ a train.__
2. Once I was_____ a rich____ man, and now I am_____ so poor.__
3.4.5. See additional lyrics

___ I've got no ex - pec - ta - tions to pass through
___ But nev - er in____ my sweet____ short life__ have I____ felt like

Verse 3:
Your heart is like a diamond.
You throw your pearls at swine.
And as I watch you leaving me
You pack my peace of mind.

Verse 4:
Our love was like the water
That splashes on a stone.
Our love was like our music,
It's here and then it's gone.

Verse 5:
So take me to the airport
And put me on a plane.
I've got no expectations
To pass through here again.

JIGSAW PUZZLE

Words and Music by
MICK JAGGER and KEITH RICHARDS

Moderately ♩ = 100

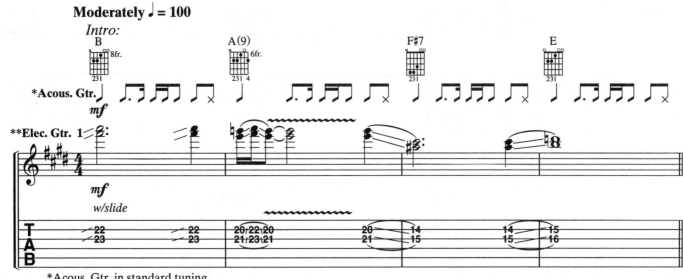

*Acous. Gtr. in standard tuning.
**Elec. Gtr. 1 in open E tuning: ⑥ = E; ⑤ = B; ④ = E; ③ = G♯; ② = B; ① = E

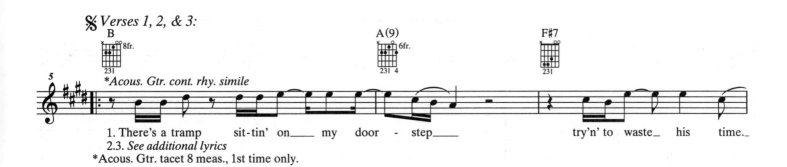

1. There's a tramp sit-tin' on__ my door - step__ try'n' to waste__ his time.__
2.3. *See additional lyrics*
*Acous. Gtr. tacet 8 meas., 1st time only.

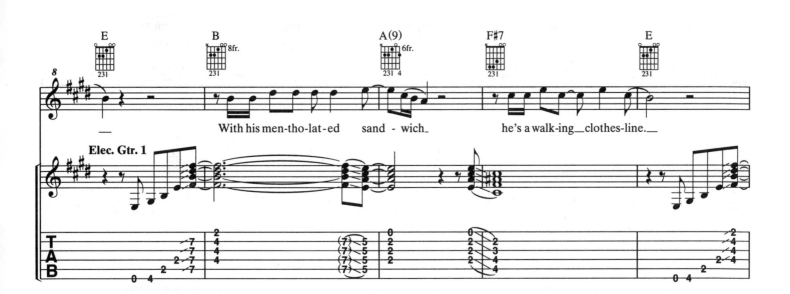

With his men-tho-lat-ed sand - wich__ he's a walk-ing__ clothes-line.__

Jigsaw Puzzle - 5 - 1
25774

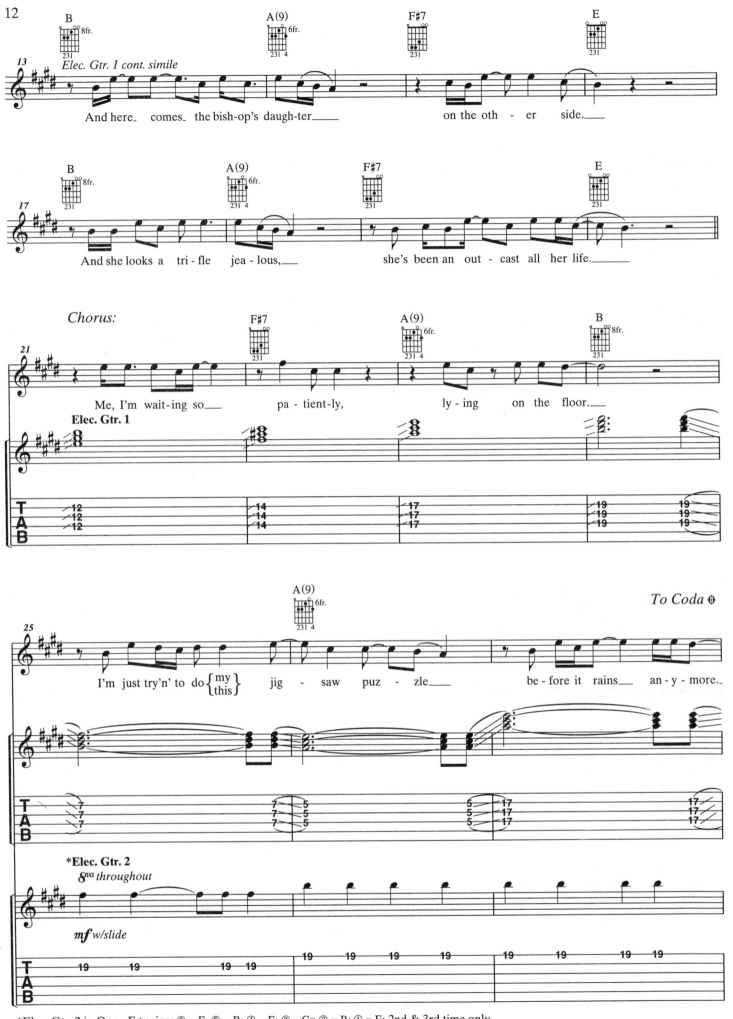

*Elec. Gtr. 2 in Open E tuning: ⑥ = E; ⑤ = B; ④ = E; ③ = G♯; ② = B; ① = E; 2nd & 3rd time only.

Jigsaw Puzzle - 5 - 2
25774

Verse 2:
Oh, the gangster looks so frightening
With his Luger in his hand.
When he gets home to his children
He's a family man.
But when it comes to the nitty-gritty,
He can shove in his knife.
Yes, he really looks quite religious,
He's been an outlaw all his life.
(To Chorus:)

Verse 3:
Oh, the singer, he looks angry
At being thrown to the lions.
And the bass player, he looks nervous
About the girls outside.
And the drummer, he's so shattered,
Tryin' to keep up time.
And the guitar players look damaged,
They've been outcasts all their lives.
(To Chorus:)

DEAR DOCTOR

Words and Music by
MICK JAGGER and KEITH RICHARDS

Verses 3 & 4:

PARACHUTE WOMAN

Words and Music by
MICK JAGGER and KEITH RICHARDS

Medium blues shuffle ♩ = 112

w/Rhy. Figs. 1 *(Acous. Gtr. 1)* **& 2** *(Acous. Gtr. 3) 1st 3 meas.*

Par - 'chute wom - an, land on me to - night.
Par - 'chute wom - an, join me for a ride.
Par - 'chute wom - an, will you blow me out?

To Coda

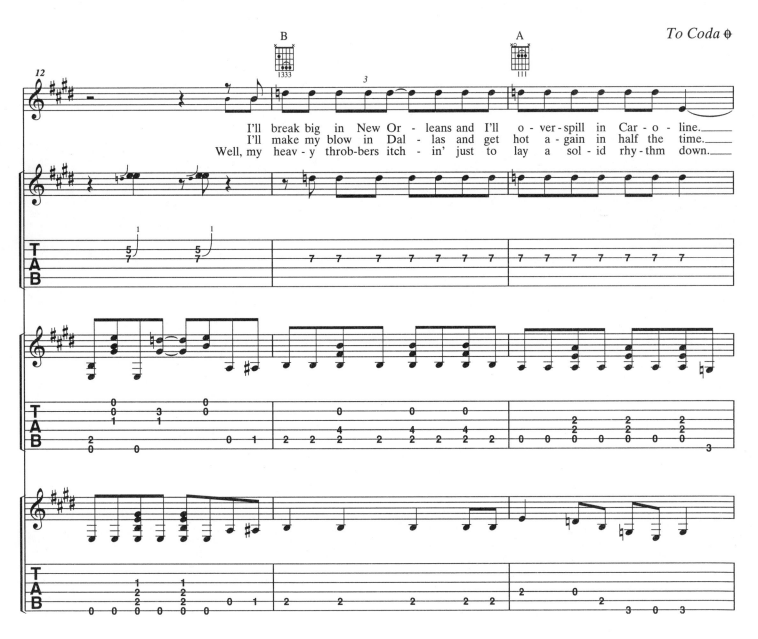

I'll break big in New Or - leans and I'll o - ver - spill in Car - o - line.
I'll make my blow in Dal - las and get hot a - gain in half the time.
Well, my heav - y throb - bers itch - in' just to lay a sol - id rhy - thm down.

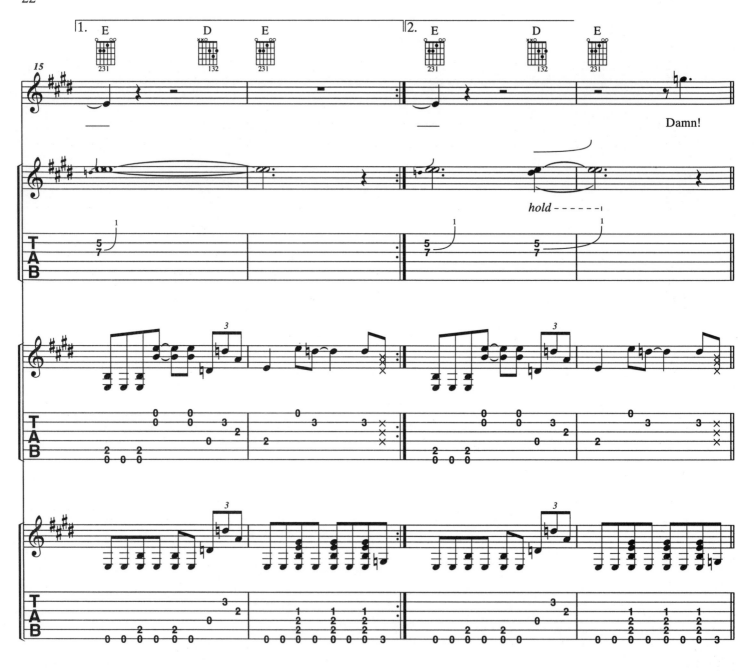

Damn!

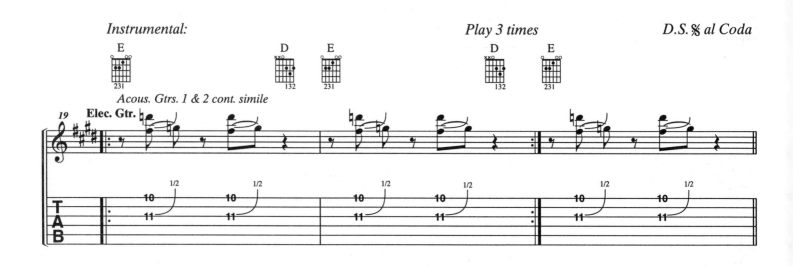

Instrumental:

Play 3 times

D.S. % al Coda

STREET FIGHTING MAN

All gtrs. in Open D tuning:
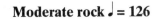

Words and Music by
MICK JAGGER and KEITH RICHARDS

Moderate rock ♩ = 126

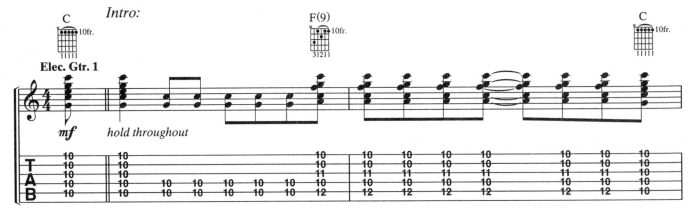

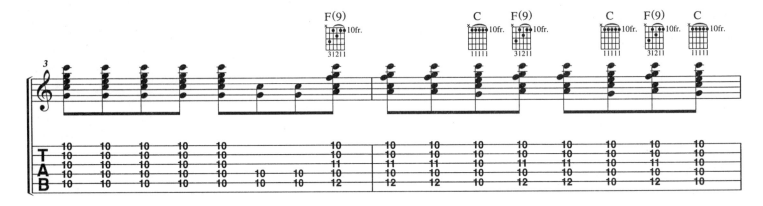

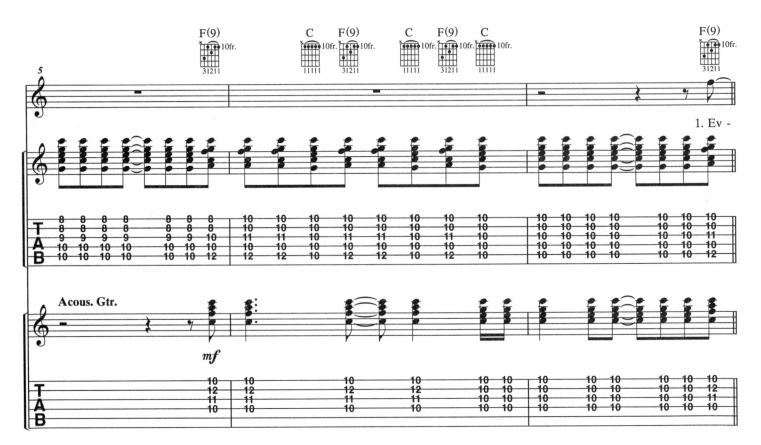

Street Fighting Man - 3 - 1
25774

Hey!___ Said my name___ is called_ Dis - tur -

- bance. I'll shout___ and scream,_ I'll kill___ the king,_ I'll rail_

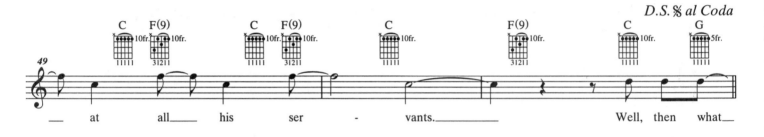

D.S. % al Coda

___ at all___ his ser - vants._____ Well, then what___

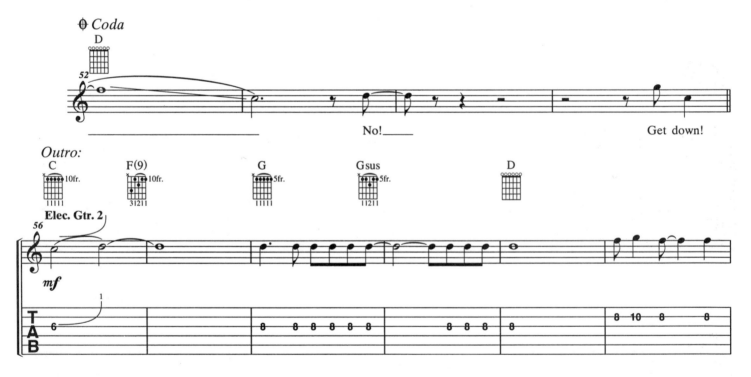

⊕ *Coda*

_____ No!___ Get down!

Outro:

Elec. Gtr. 2

mf

Repeat and fade, simile

PRODIGAL SON

Open E tuning:
⑥ = E ③ = G♯
⑤ = A ② = B
④ = D ① = E

Words and Music by
ROBERT WILKINS

Freely

Moderate 2-beat delta blues ♩ = 92

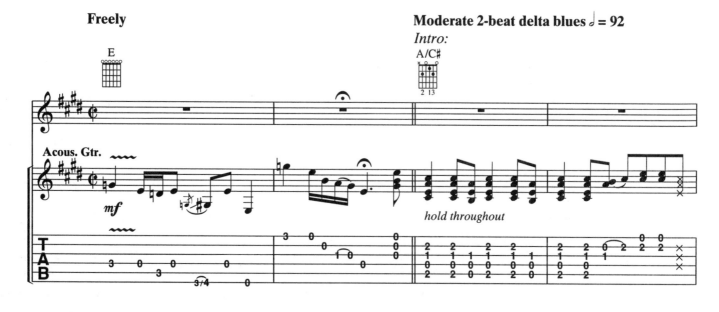

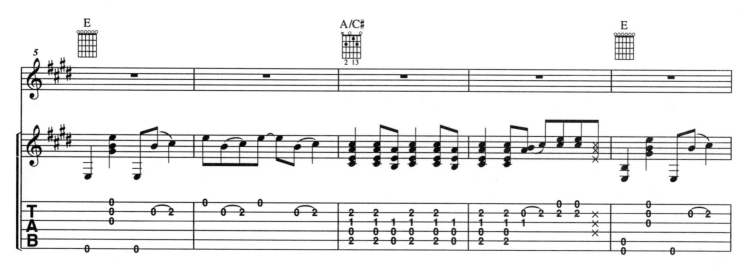

1.Well, a

Prodigal Son - 3 - 1
25774

Verse 2:
Well, poor boy spent all he had, famine come in the land,
Famine come in the land.
Spent all he had and famine come in the land.
Said, I believe I'll go and hire me to some man.
And that'll be the way I'll get along.

Verse 3:
Well, man said, "I'll give you a job for to feed my swine,
For to feed my swine.
I'll give you a job for to feed my swine."
Boy stood there and hung his head and cried
'Cause that is no way to get along.

Verse 4:
Said, "I believe I'll ride, believe I'll go back home,
Believe I'll go back home.
Believe I'll ride, believe I'll go back home
Or down the road as far as I can go.
And that'll be the way to get along."

Verse 5:
Well, father said, "See my son coming after me,
Coming home to me."
Father ran and fell down on his knees.
Said, "Sing and praise, Lord, have mercy on me,
Mercy."

Verse 6:
Oh, poor boy stood there, hung his head and cried,
Hung his head and cried.
Poor boy stood and hung his head and cried.
Said, "Father, will you look on me as a child?"
Yeah.

Verse 7:
Well, father said, "Eldest son, kill the fatted calf,
Call the family 'round.
Kill the calf and call the family 'round.
My son was lost but now he is found.
'Cause that's the way for us to get along."
Hey.

FACTORY GIRL

Words and Music by
MICK JAGGER and KEITH RICHARDS

Verse 3:
Waiting for a girl and she gets me into fights.
Waiting for a girl, we get drunk on Friday night.
She's a sight for sore eyes.
Waiting for a factory girl.

Verse 4:
Waiting for a girl, she's got stains all down her dress.
Waiting for a girl and my feet are getting wet.
She ain't come out yet.
Waiting for a factory girl.

STRAY CAT BLUES

Moderate rock ♩ = 100

Intro:

Words and Music by
MICK JAGGER and KEITH RICHARDS

Stray Cat Blues - 5 - 1
25774

A5

Play 3 times

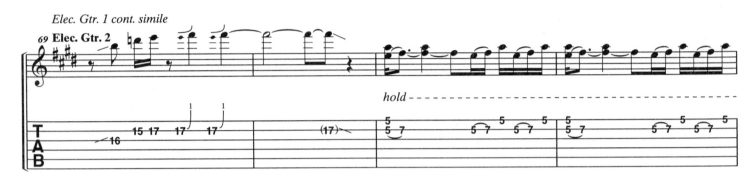

Begin fade

Fade

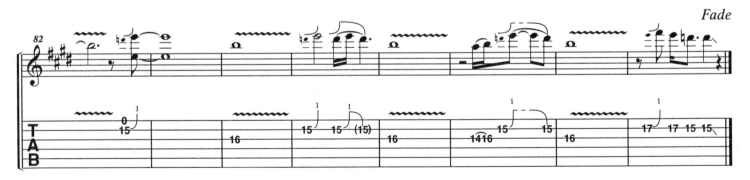

Verse 4:
You say you got a friend, that she's wilder than you.
Why don't you bring her upstairs?
If she's so wild, then she can join in too.
It's no hanging matter,
It's no capital crime.
(To Chorus:)

SALT OF THE EARTH

Words and Music by
MICK JAGGER and KEITH RICHARDS

All gtrs. in Open E tuning:
⑥ = E ③ = G#
⑤ = B ② = B
④ = E ① = E

Intro:

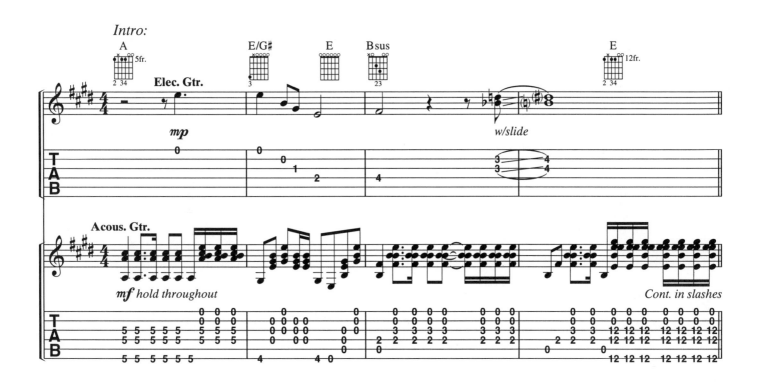

Verses 1 & 3:

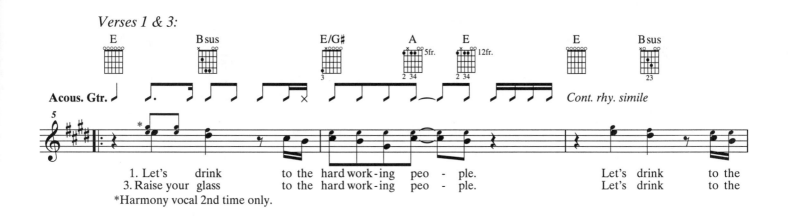

1. Let's drink to the hard work-ing peo - ple.   Let's drink to the
3. Raise your glass to the hard work-ing peo - ple.   Let's drink to the
*Harmony vocal 2nd time only.

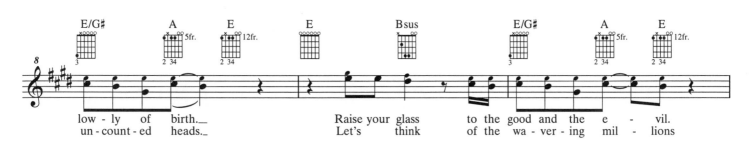

low - ly of birth.___   Raise your glass to the good and the e - vil.
un - count - ed heads.___   Let's think of the wa - ver - ing mil - lions

Salt of the Earth - 5 - 3
25774

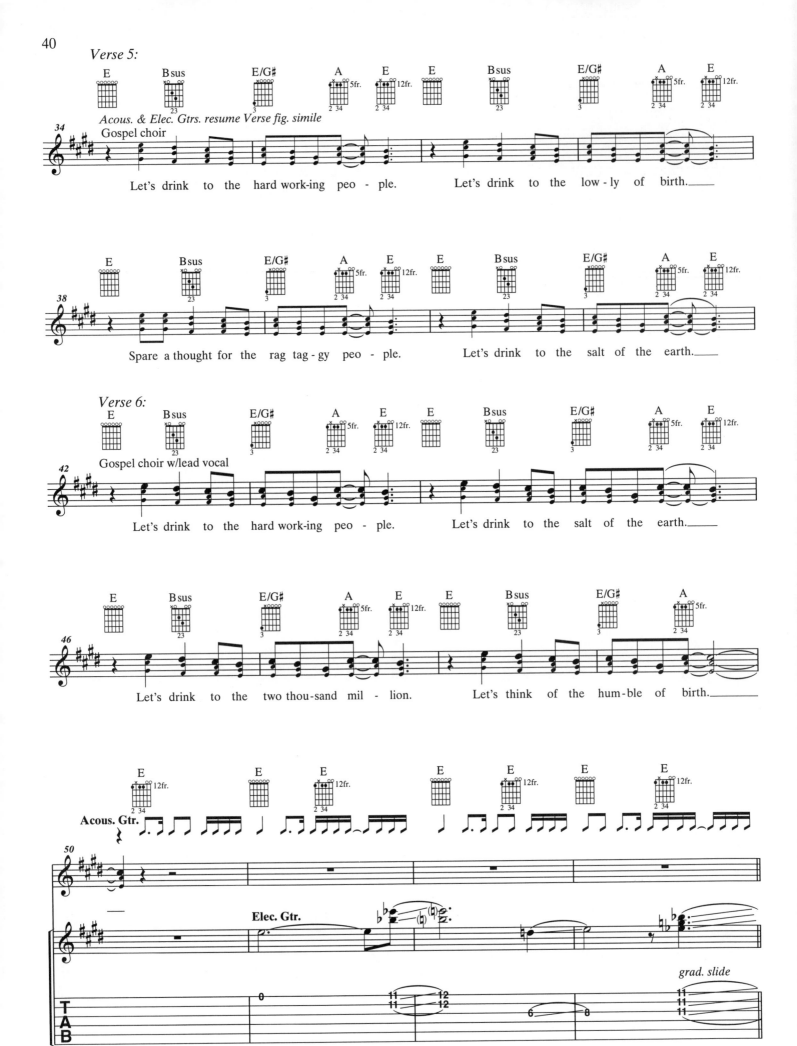

GUITAR TAB GLOSSARY **

TABLATURE EXPLANATION

READING TABLATURE: Tablature illustrates the six strings of the guitar. Notes and chords are indicated by the placement of fret numbers on a given string(s).

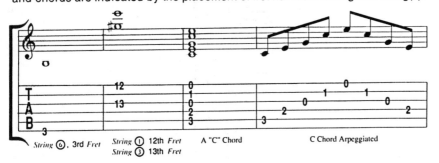

String ⑥, 3rd Fret   String ① 12th Fret   A "C" Chord   C Chord Arpeggiated
String ③ 13th Fret

BENDING NOTES

HALF STEP: Play the note and bend string one half step.*

WHOLE STEP: Play the note and bend string one whole step.

WHOLE STEP AND A HALF: Play the note and bend string a whole step and a half.

TWO STEPS: Play the note and bend string two whole steps.

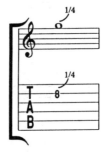

SLIGHT BEND (Microtone): Play the note and bend string slightly to the equivalent of half a fret.

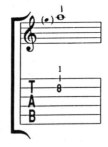

PREBEND (Ghost Bend): Bend to the specified note, before the string is picked.

PREBEND AND RELEASE: Bend the string, play it, then release to the original note.

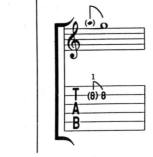

REVERSE BEND: Play the already-bent string, then immediately drop it down to the fretted note.

BEND AND RELEASE: Play the note and gradually bend to the next pitch, then release to the original note. Only the first note is attacked.

BENDS INVOLVING MORE THAN ONE STRING: Play the note and bend string while playing an additional note (or notes) on another string(s). Upon release, relieve pressure from additional note(s), causing original note to sound alone.

BENDS INVOLVING STATIONARY NOTES: Play notes and bend lower pitch, then hold until release begins (indicated at the point where line becomes solid).

UNISON BEND: Play both notes and immediately bend the lower note to the same pitch as the higher note.

DOUBLE NOTE BEND: Play both notes and immediately bend both strings simultaneously.

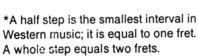

*A half step is the smallest interval in Western music; it is equal to one fret. A whole step equals two frets.

© 1990 Beam Me Up Music
c/o CPP/Belwin, Inc. Miami, Florida 33014
International Copyright Secured   Made in U.S.A.   All Rights Reserved   **By Kenn Chipkin and Aaron Stang

RHYTHM SLASHES

STRUM INDICA-TIONS: Strum with indicated rhythm.

The chord voicings are found on the first page of the transcription underneath the song title.

INDICATING SINGLE NOTES USING RHYTHM SLASHES: Very often single notes are incorporated into a rhythm part. The note name is indicated above the rhythm slash with a fret number and a string indication.

ARTICULATIONS

HAMMER ON: Play lower note, then "hammer on" to higher note with another finger. Only the first note is attacked.

LEFT HAND HAMMER: Hammer on the first note played on each string with the left hand.

PULL OFF: Play higher note, then "pull off" to lower note with another finger. Only the first note is attacked.

FRET-BOARD TAPPING: "Tap" onto the note indicated by + with a finger of the pick hand, then pull off to the following note held by the fret hand.

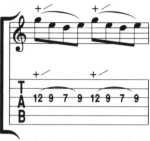

TAP SLIDE: Same as fretboard tapping, but the tapped note is slid randomly up the fretboard, then pulled off to the following note.

BEND AND TAP TECHNIQUE: Play note and bend to specified interval. While holding bend, tap onto note indicated.

LEGATO SLIDE: Play note and slide to the following note. (Only first note is attacked).

LONG GLISSAN-DO: Play note and slide in specified direction for the full value of the note.

SHORT GLISSAN-DO: Play note for its full value and slide in specified direction at the last possible moment.

PICK SLIDE: Slide the edge of the pick in specified direction across the length of the string(s).

MUTED STRINGS: A percussive sound is made by laying the fret hand across all six strings while pick hand strikes specified area (low, mid, high strings).

PALM MUTE: The note or notes are muted by the palm of the pick hand by lightly touching the string(s) near the bridge.

TREMOLO PICKING: The note or notes are picked as fast as possible.

TRILL: Hammer on and pull off consecutively and as fast as possible between the original note and the grace note.

ACCENT: Notes or chords are to be played with added emphasis.

STACCATO (Detached Notes): Notes or chords are to be played roughly half their actual value and with separation.

DOWN STROKES AND UPSTROKES: Notes or chords are to be played with either a downstroke (⊓·) or upstroke (∨) of the pick.

VIBRATO: The pitch of a note is varied by a rapid shaking of the fret hand finger, wrist, and forearm.

HARMONICS

NATURAL HARMONIC: A finger of the fret hand lightly touches the note or notes indicated in the tab and is played by the pick hand.

ARTIFICIAL HARMONIC: The first tab number is fretted, then the pick hand produces the harmonic by using a finger to lightly touch the same string at the second tab number (in parenthesis) and is then picked by another finger.

ARTIFICIAL "PINCH" HARMONIC: A note is fretted as indicated by the tab, then the pick hand produces the harmonic by squeezing the pick firmly while using the tip of the index finger in the pick attack. If parenthesis are found around the fretted note, it does not sound. No parenthesis means both the fretted note and A.H. are heard simultaneously.

TREMOLO BAR

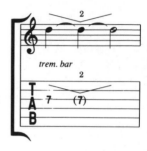

SPECIFIED INTERVAL: The pitch of a note or chord is lowered to a specified interval and then may or may not return to the original pitch. The activity of the tremolo bar is graphically represented by peaks and valleys.

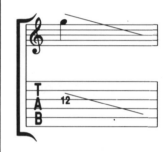

UN-SPECIFIED INTERVAL: The pitch of a note or a chord is lowered to an unspecified interval.